T0158797

June Bride isn't

just any woman…

she's Every woman

Order this book online at www.trafford.com
or email orders@trafford.com

Most Trafford titles are also available at major online book retailers.

© Copyright 2012 June Bride.
All rights reserved. No part of this publication may be reproduced, stored in a retrieval
system, or transmitted, in any form or by any means, electronic, mechanical, photocopying,
recording, or otherwise, without the written prior permission of the author.

Printed in the United States of America.

ISBN: 978-1-5536-9742-8 (sc)
ISBN: 978-1-4669-0975-5 (hc)
ISBN: 978-1-4669-0976-2 (eb)

Library of Congress Control Number: 2011963224

Trafford rev. 12/20/2011

 www.trafford.com

North America & international
toll-free: 1 888 232 4444 (USA & Canada)
phone: 250 383 6864 ✦ fax: 812 355 4082

Finally! The Truth About Marriage
An exciting new work from June Bride

You are the main reason I wrote this book. Chances are you're part of the world's population who will marry. It's 98%, you know.

Or maybe you'd rather experience marriage vicariously through the pages of this book. Either way, as your hostess for this very intimate tour of my marriage, it will be my pleasure to spill it all for you — the good and the bad.

I hope my experiences and insights will help you on you journey as you discover your own truth about marriage.

VISIT JUNE BRIDE ON THE WORLD WIDE WEB
Be sure to visit my website, http://www.JuneBrideBooks.com, where you'll find valuable resources and information about my latest adventures and musings. I guarantee you'll be entertained and learn a thing or two while you're there!

Lets stay in touch – you can send me an email message from my web site and I'll do my best to get back with you promptly whether you want to offer some feedback about the book, ask for some advice, or just let off some steam about the "Truth" in your marriage. – JB

INTRODUCTION

My husband thinks I wrote this book to complain about all of his faults. Actually, he's not all wrong. Writing is a great way to vent, but I wrote this book because I thought there might be other people out there like me--curious about marriage. What I found out is that there's no way to really know until you are married. And by then, of course, it's too late!

As your hostess for this very intimate tour of our marriage, it will be my pleasure to spill it all—the good and the bad. The actual events that took place during our time together were sometimes amusing, sometimes serious, but always filled with passion and conviction. Everything is told honestly, with a lot of hard-earned advice thrown in. I hope you find it entertaining as well as informing.

This book was written during the course of our marriage and two separations—a period of six years so far. I say "so far" because I'm still in the process of getting a divorce from him. You can check my website (www.JuneBrideBooks.com) for updates.

Occasionally, people ask me what my husband thinks of my writing this book. My answer is always the same, "He can't wait to sue me!"

THIS BOOK IS DEDICATED TO
MY BROTHER, DAVID,
WHO CONTINUES TO FILL MY HEART
WITH LOVING MEMORIES.

Contents

Wonderful Windows!
Layer for Luxury.
Showcase It!
Don't Forget Your Roots.
The Crowning Touch.
Hide it or Disguise it.
Housework--Your Hidden Enemy.
Organizing, Schmorganizing.
Welcome to the Nosyhood.

Chapter Five: It's Easy to Communicate When...

"And Another Thing..."
Should You Tell Him Everything?
Don't Ask Stupid Questions.
Learn to Negotiate...
"But I Thought You Said..."
Shut Your Clams and Listen.
Communication Lite.
Say it With Jewelry and You'll Never Be Boring!

Chapter Six: Sex and Stuff

"Why Couldn't I Have Married a Nymphomaniac?"
His Sex Life Improved Every Time He...
A Massage By Hand Made the Sex More Grand.
When His Minimum Met Her Maximum...

ACKNOWLEDGEMENTS

I would like to thank everyone who has helped me realize this dream - my family, my friends and many others, without whom this book wouldn't have been written and published. I'd especially like to thank my Mother for her love and generous support always. Mom, I'm proud and grateful to be your daughter. No one could ever be more loving. And you're still the most intelligent person I know! Thanks also to my Father with his wonderful sense of humor. I also want to let my four beautiful sisters know how much I love them and how much they mean to me.

I am also grateful to two of my greatest mentors, John Taylor and Leona Hershkowitz. John, words cannot express the feelings I have for you for being so many things to me. Your friendship, wisdom, patience, love and confidence in me have helped me mature as a woman and human being. For all your kindness and generosity, the only thing you asked for in return was that I help someone else the way that you've helped me. Please know that every day I do my best to keep that promise I made to you.

Leona, from you I learned how to stand up for myself as a woman and also benefitted from your contribution in my development as a writer. These are gifts I will treasure always.

Finally, a very special thank you to Mark, I hope you know how much I love you and how much I appreciate your help.

Chapter One: Getting to Know You...

My Mother told me that when she married my Father she thought he had all his own teeth and he thought she was a natural blonde. But false teeth and bottled hair color were just the beginning of their dirty little secrets. We know they're not alone, don't we?

Boy Meets Girl.
And according to my husband, a girl with 19 personalities. So I'm 18 times the woman he expected! He didn't always judge me so harshly...

Love was in the air. The air at the flea market. Yep, that's where I met my husband. We sometimes joked that he found his whole life there. After all, that's where he met me, bought our dog and hired the real estate agent who found our home. Andre worked there on the weekends, and I was selling floral arrangements I'd made to supplement an income I didn't have. That was the first and last day of my sales career, but my life would be forever changed. It started with an invitation to a jazz club.

Within two months of meeting Andre, I fell madly in love and knew that he was the man I wanted to marry. On what did I base this "rash" decision? Well, I've always loved a gentleman, and he was that. On our very first date, he brought me flowers. He opened all doors and let me walk in first.

My point is that whatever special attention he gave me, it did *not* go unnoticed. And you know what? That part of his personality never changed! Right up until the time I left him he gave me flowers, and gifts and cards with sweet, hand-written messages inside.

Most importantly, though, a genuine kindness emanated from Andre. In the short time I'd known him, he had helped me find clients for a new business I was trying to start, fixed the air conditioner in my car, worked on a co-worker's car at my request, and moved me twice.

This was all while he held a full-time job, in addition to his part-time job, and also went to school at night! If that type of person doesn't earn your respect, who does?

Seven months later we had my fantasy wedding. I didn't have to look to other men anymore because I had it all in my own backyard. Moreover, the man had chosen to *marry* me, not just date me for Eternity (as had some others). He liked to get credit for that. And he did.

Meet the Family.

My husband and I both come from large families--six children in each. Andre's Father was an international attorney who was very loved and respected by my husband. Tragically, he died when Andre was only nine years old. To date, his Mother has not remarried.

Meanwhile, in my military home, you'd think Mother was prepping her girls to marry royalty. She spent her evenings sewing beautiful dresses for us, and both parents were strict enforcers of good behavior and manners. After my parent's marriage of 21 years ended, they both married other people. And divorced again.

Two months before our wedding, Andre stood in the doorway of our recently purchased home with the cutest puppy in the world and announced, "Meet Jackie!" I don't know if the word "spoiled" accurately describes her. Suffice it to say that we didn't sleep alone and the third party was not a mistress. In fact, it was so much the opposite that my husband added "The Anti-sex" to her list of nicknames.

Our Tabby cat, Lucy, has been my little friend since she was born in my bedroom closet 18 years ago and she rounds out our nuclear family. Our "kids," as my husband called them, were treated like the children we never had.

Fast Forward to the Wedding.

"Are we going to have a honeymoon?" I asked my husband of ten minutes. We were still at the Church posing for our wedding pictures. "Yes," he whispered in my ear. What a relief! I couldn't see taking a ten-day honeymoon in Panama with nothing but two round-trip plane tickets and $300 in cash, but as far as I knew, that's all we had.

How did *that* happen? Well, my then-fiancée handled the money for the wedding. The problem was resolved in his mind by borrowing his Mother's credit card. Wait 'til you read how *that* played out.

First, though, a free tip from June Bride. Be assertive about telling anyone who is in a position to give you special treatment that you're on your honeymoon. There's likely to be some freebies in it for you. Here's how Yours Truly got two First-class upgrades for the first leg of our trip to Miami.

After I watched the last of the passengers receive their boarding passes, I walked up to the ticket agent behind the counter and politely made my pitch. I said something like, "Hi, my husband and I are on our honeymoon (big smile). I wondered if we could move to First Class if there are any extra seats." Sometimes First Class seats are available even if Coach is full, and most airline personnel are glad to accommodate their customers if they can.

A few computer keyboard strokes later, everybody was happy. We sank into roomy, leather seats and the ticket agent got to feel good about herself by doing something nice for the newlyweds. I thought about how I would include this in my book for ya'll as we toasted each other with complimentary champagne and ate from real china.

Once in Panama, we rented a car and drove to the first stop on our itinerary--a seaside villa belonging to our new sister-in-law's family. It overlooked a private beach with sparkling black sand.

Two days later, we felt exhilarated as we drove into Panama City. I found a bottle of wine left over from the night before and continued celebrating. It was the best wine I'd ever had, and I was swigging it straight from the bottle. I didn't care if it *was* 8:00 in the morning!

As we explored the city, Andre decided it wasn't fair that only one of us got pampered at a beauty salon in preparation for our wedding. So right then and there, he insisted I get a manicure and pedicure. As we popped into a nearby salon, Andre read a magazine while I finally got what I deserved.

Andre's Best Man had gifted him with a massage, manicure and pedicure the morning of our wedding. Not as wild an experience as your average bachelor party perhaps, but a perfect alternative for someone who didn't want one anyway.

"What Did You Call Me?!"

This is the worst thing that happened to me on my honeymoon. And the first time I thought of divorce. It began with Andre's Mother's credit card. Even though Andre was a registered cardholder, local businesses *could* not or *would* not verify it for our use. Although it wasn't a problem at the hotel, it *was* a problem just about everywhere else. The first place we found out it wasn't welcome was at the car rental agency. When we returned the car and Andre tried to pay for it with the card, the woman at the counter refused to accept it.

Meanwhile, I was sitting outside with our suitcases. It was still an hour before check in time at our hotel across the street, so we planned on eating lunch first. As Andre walked out of the rental agency, I noticed the representative calling for him to come back. Since he was not responding, I thought he didn't hear her. I told him that she was trying to get his attention. He told me to ignore her, grabbed some suitcases, and ordered me to follow him on foot. When I persisted, he said, "Come on—a__hole!"

If there was ever a time in my life when I was absolutely, positively shocked, that was it! Andre and I had barely even had a disagreement prior to our wedding, let alone anything like that!

As I turned the street corner trying to catch up with him (luggage in tow), I said, "How could you call me an a__hole on our honeymoon?!" I don't know if Andre heard me, but a middle-aged, male passerby obviously caught the last part. He looked at me with disgust and said, "Hey, lady! I don't know how they talk in *your* country, but we don't use language like that here." Talk about adding insult to injury!

I hurried on and found my husband seated at an outdoor table at a nearby restaurant. I was crying as the waitress came up to take our order. With tears streaming down my face, I again asked Andre how he could say that to me.

He explained that he didn't mean it; he was just trying to get my attention. He was sorry. He may have *been* sorry, but not as sorry as I wanted him to be.

After lunch, still trying to recover from the verbal blow, Andre and I continued walking the streets. I was admiring some earrings in one of the shops when the woman from the car rental agency suddenly appeared. She beckoned my husband, and she wasn't alone; there was a gentleman accompanying her.

The woman quietly asked Andre to come back and pay the bill in cash. I don't know exactly what he told them, but the man and woman left without incident. With that, we called our new brother-in-law--a Panamanian attorney. He returned to the agency with us and paid for the rental himself. If we ever paid him back, I never heard about it.

Since we were limited to cash spending, we found ourselves in a bit of a spot. I *could* look on the bright side, I guess. We had no need to drop because we couldn't shop. We didn't gain weight because we could barely afford to eat. And we were spared the possible back strain from carrying all the stuff we could have bought at an 85% discount! It wasn't long before we began to hatch a plan to fly to Vegas on that card. Did we do it?

In the end, we didn't have the guts. At least I didn't; Andre probably would have. I didn't know his Mother very well, but I knew her well enough to know that she would have taken a switch to that boy had we done that. As it was, we took the next available flight back home, leaving a few days early.

The Aftershock.

This occurred for me when I found out that Andre was capable of being so mean. About the same time, I suspect, Andre came to find out I wasn't kidding about how much I hate cooking and cleaning. It's real.

Even things I thought to be absolute truths about my husband turned out to be flawed to some degree. And in some cases, the outright opposite. For example, Andre, my then-fiancée, made it sound like *he* was the financially responsible one in his last relationship. He complained bitterly about the spending habits of his ex, but that wasn't quite the whole story. As I discovered over time.

In the beginning of *our* relationship, I was convinced that Andre could--and would--handle our finances responsibly. After all, he had purchased two homes prior to ours, traded in the stock market, had $12,000 in a savings account and drove a new truck that was financed.

All I can say is, when it comes to money, don't assume. I wish I had asked him to share credit reports. And talk in detail about how and by whom our income would be distributed. What we discovered too late was that we both wanted to make those decisions. In fact, there are a lot of things we failed to discover about each other before we got married.

Like the things I'm not willing to do--married or not. Cooking and cleaning on a regular basis, for one. You'll also not find me raking the leaves or doing any sort of house or car maintenance.

Andre, though, is a high-energy type of individual who enjoys keeping busy. He gets up in the morning and goes all day. Just to make things interesting, I guess, he married a low-energy person who abhors physical labor. And the poor thing had no idea how much I sleep--probably 40% more than the average person.

"I'm tired of coming home to a corpse," he communicated to me one evening. I don't blame him; I hated it, too. Sometimes I would come home from work and take my usual nap which may have lasted until 5:30 the next morning.

That's one reason I don't have children. When I call my dog to nap with me, she's down for the count. She never whines, cries or refuses to go to bed. I can't stand chaos around me, so I purposely stage my life to avoid it.

Another constant in my life that Andre couldn't stand is my procrastination. The most recent example I can think of is when I decided to take a defensive driving course. You know, to get rid of a speeding ticket? I got permission from the Court and received 90 days to attend a six-hour class.

First, I decided that I was going to take the course offered at a comedy club (they do that in Texas). I checked into where it was being held, but never got around to actually going there. Then, I was going to attend a driving school close to the house. I guess I waited too long there, too, because by the time I got around to driving by, they were out of business.

On the eve of the 88th day, I finally rented a six-hour video course from Blockbuster's. I wound up staying up half the night with that thing!

Procrastination is an irritating habit, but I think it's small-time compared to my husband's I'll call them "occasional memory lapses." Here's a pretty appalling example.

11

At one point, we decided to sell our home and buy a townhouse. The loan officer was completing the application according to the information my husband was giving him. The next question was, "Have you ever had a bankruptcy?" "No," I answered in my mind. "Yes," I heard my husband say. What?! I looked over at him in disbelief.

For a whole year, he'd chastised me for the way *I* handle *my* finances! Not once had he ever mentioned that he'd had a bankruptcy. Forget the insult, the hypocrisy was unbelievable.

I guess the biggest surprise of all to me concerning marriage is that now there was someone else second-guessing my decisions. I couldn't continue doing things my own way even though they still made sense to me.

Andre and I were both very independent people when we met, and we were both willing to fight for what we wanted. When our ideas clashed, it became a power struggle--with people becoming unreasonable in the process.

Like with Jackie. Andre wouldn't let her go anywhere with us in the car--except to the vet. It follows that every time she got in the car, she thought she was going to a place she hates.

Therein lies my argument for letting her come along if we were just running errands and the like. Since she wouldn't always know where she was going--could be to the park--maybe she wouldn't be so anxious about the trip. Andre used the same argument in reverse. He didn't want her to expect that she was going with us every time we left the house.

That was the first sniff I got that my husband could be so unreasonable about something that seemed so clear to me. As much as I thought I knew about him, it wasn't enough. I hadn't seen that stubborn side of him. All in all, I'd say Andre managed to hide about 37% of his personality. And I made it easy for him.

Here's the trap. In the beginning of a relationship, it's natural to focus on one or more aspects of an individual. If you're falling in love, these aspects are going to be favorable. From there, it's an easy stretch to imagine that those qualities represent the person as a whole. There's even a name for it--it's called "The Halo Effect."

When I first met Andre, I thought he was sweet and kind. Since I didn't know of any *glaring* liabilities at that point, I formed my initial opinion of him as good.

I quickly came to assume that anyone *that* good had to be good marriage material, as well. In fact, the Halo Effect was so much in force at the time of our wedding, I simply couldn't find fault with the man! Now, of course, it's easy.

Don't Expect Perfection and You Won't Be Disappointed.

I used to have this dream that if I could just find my one true love, everything else in my life would fall into place. Indulging in the fantasy that a husband was going to rescue me served as a stress reliever many a time. There would be no more problems. And if there were, we would overcome them together.

What I didn't factor in, though, is that some of the problems I have today are *because* of my husband. And ditto for him. It's logical to assume that most everything we do singularly will affect us as a couple.

There are plenty of things Andre did that failed to live up to my expectations. I'll start with something small. I didn't care for the way he dressed.

One day I was watching him exit the living room and was aghast by what I saw. His outfit made Robinson Crusoe look like he'd just left Brooks Brothers! But, if wearing raggedy jeans and old t-shirts complete with holes made him happy, who was I to judge?

He didn't always like my sense of style, either. Basically, I liked him to dress more preppy, and he liked me to dress more casually.

But looks aren't everything. And thank goodness, because you're going to see things you never thought you'd see. You're also going to become painfully familiar with all of his hygiene habits. Only *after* the wedding will you find out exactly how often he brushes his teeth and *if* he showers every day.

There were *significant* disappointments, however. I expected Andre to finish college like he said he would, but he quit during our engagement. I encouraged him to go back after we married, but he insisted we couldn't afford it. I have little sympathy for this excuse since I found a way to pay for my college education. I thought he had the tenacity to finish, and I felt let down to find out otherwise, for obvious reasons.

Although Andre said he was proud of my aspirations, I don't think he appreciated the time and sacrifice involved to achieve my goals as a writer. And I became twice as vigilant to be successful as I watched him flounder career-wise.

Furthermore, he did nothing to facilitate my efforts to accomplish my dream. In fact, he got in the way. By spending too much money and making me work. If he would have just agreed to let me work part-time, that would have been a big help. It seems to me that he was not as supportive as a husband should be.

But by far, the biggest expectation my husband failed to meet was to always treat me with kindness and respect. I knew we would have arguments occasionally, but I never thought they would turn into something barbaric. Andre began saying horrible things to me. Things that I couldn't forget, even though I did forgive. The main reason I married Andre was because he was so kind to me. Take that away, and I'd want to leave.

Andre, too, claimed to be disillusioned. He told me he thought he'd married someone who was a team player--someone who would work with him to accomplish goals together. Amazing! I felt the same disappointment.

At least I did my part by not spending money. He even admitted that I never asked him for anything. I knew if I did, I'd end up paying for it myself somewhere down the line.

One thing Andre wanted me to know was his surprise regarding the amount of time I spent with two of my sisters, Diane and Nancy. And he was particularly disenchanted to discover how often my parents came to visit. He said it was every six weeks, but it was only four or five times a year. They live 400 miles away.

I guess neither of us felt that we got the spousal support we expected. We each had our own agendas as individuals, and I don't think we thought much about those being interrupted by marriage. Looking back, we should have known better.

What it's Like--Really!

Imagine yourself returning to work after your honeymoon. If that's not bad enough, you're told that your position was cut during your absence. You drive home with the anticipation of going back to bed.

As you turn into your subdivision, though, you notice your husband heading out of it. You roll down your window and ask him what he's doing home at 10:00 in the morning. He says he's just been fired and is on his way to the unemployment office. He invites you to join him and you do. Just two little surprises that jump-started our married life. And they continued.

New horrors--I mean *habits*--surfaced all the time. I'd see Andre's cigarette ashes on the end table in the living room. I also found them in coffee grounds, in my shower, toilet, sink, vanity, rug, bed and dresser. My husband also left coffee stains on the carpet on both sides of the console in my new car because he drank coffee all the time. He even got *me* drinking coffee like a long-distance trucker! It wasn't hard to pick up each others habits--for better or worse.

I knew we wouldn't agree on *everything*, but the surprise is when you can't agree on *anything*. Like what kind of detergent to use. Who knew a man would be so attached to the detergent he grew up with? I, on the other hand, don't think much about detergent. If it's on sale that day and it's easy to carry, it's my favorite.

One day we went on a two-hour shopping trip together. I *knew* I shouldn't have invited him. Even before we left the house, we disagreed about where we would go. I had planned to take his *Radio Shack brand* camcorder to Radio Shack to get a new battery for it. And since it was my idea to replace it in the first place, I thought I should handle it the way I wanted. Not when Andre was around! He argued me down until I went to Wal-Mart.

What he didn't realize is that shopping is a personal experience for me. I like to relax and take my time in comfortable surroundings. I don't want to drive from warehouse to warehouse looking for something they don't sell. For the few dollars that may be saved in the event they do have the item, it's *still* not worth it to me. I prefer to go straight to the source and get it over with. It's part of my continuing effort to lead as stress-free a life as possible.

There were occasions, of course, when I just *knew* that what we were discussing was not going to come to a positive conclusion no matter how many rounds we went. We didn't *have* to agree on every little thing, and we certainly didn't. What we *did* have to do was resolve our differences or learn to live with them.

For example, there's one long-standing dispute we had since the beginning of our marriage. It was a small request my husband made of me, but I'd never been able to accommodate him. He wanted me to stop using the garbage disposal. Well, I happen to *love* the garbage disposal, and I was not about to stop using it. And I had a very good reason--it's more sanitary than letting garbage rot in the kitchen closet.

But then Andre had a point, too. He claimed that the food would clog the pipes. I argued that chopping up food small enough to flow through those pipes is the job of a garbage disposal, but he wouldn't budge. No problem; I just used it when he wasn't around.

Sometimes I felt like I married The King of Denial. Here's a case in point.

I'd told Andre ever since we got our puppy that she shouldn't be eating table scraps. When she got fat, you're not going to believe who he blamed it on. He was absolutely serious when he suggested that *the neighbors* were throwing food over the back fence to her behind our backs! He refused to admit that it had anything to do with the pizza, hot dogs, ice cream, meatloaf and creamed spinach he fed her. And the girl can eat from a fork as well as any four-year-old, if that tells you anything.

It got to the point where I had to fight to keep my *own* food. I almost lost my meatballs to her one night. I was looking forward to eating a leftover spaghetti dinner and those meatballs were a big part of it. Still, Andre snatched one out of the refrigerator and gave it to her, telling me I didn't need all of them.

Basically, I wasn't happy with my husband every day. And I wasn't happy to be married every day. And the same was true for Andre, of course. Most days we felt blessed to have each other, but some days...

We both had a vision of what married life would bring. Mine included hosting fancy dinner parties with lots of friends, spending our summers in the Hamptons and the winters in our cozy condo in Aspen.

However, that lifestyle was not synonymous with what my husband and I could afford. Andre had a job that left him so exhausted once he got home at 7:30 in the evening he could barely stay awake long enough to move from the couch to the bed. And I, too, did not find that I had enough oomph to go grocery shopping after work, let alone plan a dinner party for Saturday night.

So what went on when we were at home? Well, one night I walked into our computer room and the first thing that grabbed my attention was a woman's G-string clad rear. Oh, the rear wasn't in the room, it was on the computer screen. And I was surprised to see it. After I refocused, I asked my husband what any self-respecting wife would,

"Are we paying for this?!" He assured me we weren't, and the issue was dead as far as I was concerned.

Honestly, I didn't care that Andre loitered *outside* those websites if that's what he needed to make it through his day. He escaped to another dimension, however, when he demanded I own up to an Internet picture he stumbled across of a half-naked blonde!

I couldn't wait to see what *I* knew was a look-alike, so I asked Andre to find it again. He said he doubted he could, but all his diligence paid off a whole 45 seconds later. I must say I was stunned at the resemblance! Her breasts came as close to mine as any I've ever seen. I revisited this issue with him again to remind myself on how we resolved it. He told me he was still waiting for a confession.

Ever had "buyer's remorse"? Well, marriage is kind of like that. There were times when I wanted to give Andre back to his Mother for a refund. He had a private world of mail orders, court orders and evading orders that I found out about over time. I'll explain more about that later. For now, know that some of his choices in the past began catching up to him.

My life wasn't as exciting as it was when I was an active single, but I was more at peace. That's one thing I can say for marriage--it's settling. Or at least it was for me. I felt like I had a sense of security I haven't felt since I left Mommy's womb. Andre and I didn't go to fancy restaurants very often, but we did fall into bed together every night feeling wanted and loved. Whoever said the best things in life are free is right!

When you come right down to it, marriage is the comfort of being wrapped in your favorite robe. It's also the feeling of your veins popping up in your neck from anger. On an average day, though, it's somewhere in between.

Actually being *in* a marriage, I can understand why the divorce rate is so high. The problems begin when that package you bought (into) starts to unwrap itself. The unwrapping could reveal anything from minor disappointments to a complete metamorphosis of the person. Expect just about anything, including this...

Help! I Married My Father.
I vowed to marry someone just the opposite. Instead, I found Dad's long lost twin. I love him, but the world's greatest husband and Father he was not. I don't know what amazes me more--the fact that my husband and my

Father have so much in common, or that I didn't notice the similarities until after I married Andre!

Neither my husband nor my Dad drink alcohol very often, but you'd never find them without a cup of coffee. They also both smoke cigarettes--with no intention of quitting.

And their personalities! They're both charismatic extroverts. My Dad is probably the most outgoing person I've ever known. And my husband doesn't have a shy bone in his body, either. Since I *am* shy, I wanted an outgoing husband. Well, I got one--just like Dad. And if you believe in Astrology, you'll love this one--they're both born under the same sign!

My Father has a great sense of humor. It's usually at someone else's expense, but he does joke around a lot. Andre, too, uses his wit to amuse himself. That, also, was usually at the expense of someone else--me! It wasn't a problem, though. I just gave it right back to him. Sometimes it was the only way we could get through to each other.

Stubborn is another word that comes to mind when I think of the two of them. This is my Mother's Miracle story about my Dad, but it could just as well have been my husband.

It begins with a family trip across the United States that could have ended in disaster. When my Father took a transfer overseas, we traveled by car across the country to catch the plane. There was plenty of time to get there, but my Dad chose to put pressure on himself despite my Mother's objections. He drove all day and all night until he fell asleep at the wheel and ran off the road. He totaled a car carrying a wife and three children under five years old. Here's the Miracle part. No one was seriously injured and we arrived at our destination on schedule. Ego before reason? Sounds all too familiar.

That's not to say that Dad doesn't have some good qualities because like my Mother says, "No one is *all* bad-- not even your Father." Here is something I especially like about my Dad.

I remember how affectionate he was with my Mother. He would wrap his arms around her waist and snuggle into her as she was washing the dishes, for example. And he always kissed her before leaving the house. Their problems began when he became affectionate with too many people (of the female persuasion).

Here's where my Dad and my husband part company. I want to make it clear that my husband abhors infidelity. I never suspected him of this practice, and I didn't expect to. If there's one thing I was confident about in Andre, it was his loyalty.

One very sad thing that my husband and my Dad have in common is the premature death of their Father. My Dad lost his Father to pneumonia. He was the oldest of three children left behind with a Mother who wasn't equipped to cope. At 11 years old, my Father became unruly, and was punished often.

My husband, too, suffered the devastation of a little boy torn apart by circumstance. But when Andre spoke of his Father's death, it was always from his Mother's perspective. He never really told me how *he* felt, except that his family's attempts to protect him from learning that his Father was dying were in vain. He already knew. At the same time, he would hide his own fears.

If, then, anger comes from unresolved fear--as is widely suggested--perhaps the greatest commonality of them all is not so surprising. It involves two grown men with childish tempers. Dad has a very short fuse, and my husband's got shorter all the time, I noticed.

Much to their family's demise, both men could be verbally abusive. I truly believe that these men have precious little sense of the catastrophic damage this single behavior causes. I can still recall every unkind name my Father ever called me. And although he was complimentary at times, the insults are so much more ingrained in my memory. I guess that happens to everyone; we remember the negative the most because it obviously affects us the most.

Basically, I wish my Father had realized how important his words really were to me. And 30 years later, here I am wishing the same thing for the man I married.

Does history repeat itself? In so many areas, I think the evidence here is hard to ignore.

So, is Marriage the Key to Happiness?

It all depends on whether or not you've done your homework. Do you even *know* the man? Are you sure? What motivates him? Is he motivated at all? If so, towards what? Do you share his lifelong dream to live out in the boonies and fish all day? Will he support your decision to go on vacation with your sister? How will he react if you go anyway? Is he an impulsive decision-maker? Or does he procrastinate so long that the decisions make themselves?

Exactly how interested *is* he in helping you to become all that you can be? Is he smart enough to provide for your financial future? Will he do it? And, my personal favorite, is he good enough to be the Father of your precious child? If you're going to make a mistake with a man, don't make it here.

And you--are you the type who needs emotional support for a hangnail? Seriously think about what *you* need from a relationship and ask yourself if he's fulfilling it. It's a pretty sure bet that if he ain't fulfilling it now, he ain't gonna be fulfilling it in the future!

Next, are you quick to adapt to somebody being in your face all the time? Because you're practically going to *have* to if you're married. Personally, I don't mind being alone and even enjoy solitude. As you might expect, Andre is just the opposite. So much so that he often choose to work on his days off if I wasn't at home! I don't get it.

It sounds like an oxymoron, but you *can* be married and lonely at the same time. Like losing contact with single friends. It's not deliberate; it's just pretty much a natural progression.

One birthday, for example, I was a little upset because I didn't get cards from anyone outside of my family. Thank goodness Andre was there to sympathize. He said, "Did you really expect any? You don't even return their phone calls!" He was right (I *hate* that). It *was* my fault. I'll do better once this book is finished.

"I'm moody at home," this young, married co-worker told me. I never would have guessed it from her personality at work, but then isn't that all of us? I know I'm more temperamental at home than I am at the office.

By the time my husband and I got home from work, we were ready to be ourselves--and, depending on our day--maybe even someone *worse* than ourselves, and we still had to love each other.

Whether it's a "woman thing" or a "man thing," there are going to be times (oh, are there going to be times), when you're both difficult to live with. Sometimes the best you can hope for is that your mood swings don't clash.

My advice is that only one of you get an attitude at a time. This leaves one partner available to comfort and reassure the other. And it freed my husband from focusing on his own negative energy!

Chapter Two: Relatives and Other Marriage Busters

My husband was my best friend. Since he kept me from everyone else, I guess that's no shocker. That may be a slight exaggeration, but sometimes I wondered. He certainly made no secret of the fact that he hated my family.

"That Bitch in Minneapolis."

Unfortunately, not an unreasonable term of endearment bestowed on my Grandmother by my Mother. My Grandmother started it by referring to my Mother as "The Foreigner" (Mother is from England). If there was ever a classic hate-hate relationship among Mothers- and Daughters-in-law, this was it. And it lasted over 20 years.

I got along with my Mother-in-Law okay, but I didn't want to see her as often as my husband did. I encouraged Andre to visit her alone, whenever possible. If we were asking for money, though, he made me go with him.

That's one thing I can say about my husband's Mother. She was very generous with us. She even bought us appliances for our new home.

More often than not, it was *my* family that could be a source of misery for us. It's partly my fault. I guess I said, "Can you believe that bitch?" one too many times when speaking of my sisters because Andre used to lecture me on being taken advantage of by them.

I'm not saying that a man shouldn't be his wife's greatest protector--that part is wonderful--but his suspicions regarding my sisters were just the beginning. He's also made mincemeat out of my friends.

I didn't see what he could possibly have had against them, anyway. Most of them don't even live in our town, and he barely knew the ones who do. Every time my husband made a negative remark about my family or friends it hurt me. I adore them all, and I doubt if I could be happy without them.

Thus, when my husband questioned their motives, his "advice" was an argument waiting to happen. Not only because he insulted my intelligence, but also because he made himself a higher authority. I would rather have seen my husband's passion to protect me tempered with a little more trust in my judgment.

But spouses are not the only ones who can ruin a good partnership. Just because your marriage is none of their business, doesn't mean the relatives are going to stay out of it. Especially if you're feeding them all the bad stuff. This was my problem, and my husband knew it.

My Mother and I are very close, so she got an earful when I got upset. Then she got upset. The worst part is that she would still be holding a grudge long after I'd forgiven him.

It's not that I told her just the bad stuff, I told her a lot of things. It was wrong--and definitely unhealthy for my marriage--but I just couldn't seem to quit doing it. Maybe it's the writer in me; I have an insatiable need to communicate my feelings. And since I confide in my Mother a lot, things are bound to come out.

I *did* quit asking for her advice, though. And before she offered it, she'd ask me if I wanted it first. I'd always say yes because she is so smart. Then, when I'd heard what she had to say, I'm sorry I asked her after all. Sometimes I wish I just could have kept my big mouth shut.

The Angry Partner.
I was horrified the first time my husband told me to shut my mouth. And I was just as horrified when I said it to him.

During the course of our marriage, we said a lot of crummy things to each other. He told me I have buck teeth, beady eyes and was too stupid to be his wife. I told him he was too dumb to keep his mouth shut, was totally irresponsible and I had married him on the rebound.

I guess my sister was right when she told me that my husband and I brought out the worst in each other. Andre and I *both* have tempers and when they ignited at the same time, watch out! We were a matching pair of lunatics. I'm not proud to say that we did not always exercise control over our mouths once our tempers got the best of us.

Believe it or not, Andre and I never had a disagreement of any consequence until after we got engaged. After we got married, we argued some, but I can't say it was a lot. It was the intensity of the arguments that bothered me the most.

If we were in the mood to yell, no reason was too small, it seemed. For example, Andre came home from work one day and we were having a normal conversation in the kitchen. All of a sudden he shrieked, "Is it too much to ask you to make another pot of coffee after you drink all mine?!" Knowing that's one of his pet peeves, I apologized immediately. I had planned on making another pot, but had gotten interrupted by the phone and then forgot about it. The only reason a 45-minute argument ensued after that was due to his nasty tone.

And when it came to reaching back in history for those past criticisms that were good enough to use again and again, we both had our favorites.

On the subject of money, for example. Andre liked to remind me of the time I bought $60 worth of coat hangers (I was trying to organize my closet). Likewise, I couldn't let him forget how he got suckered into paying $169 for what was suppose to be a $39 discount carpet cleaning.

"How Much is it Going to Cost Me to Get a Divorce?!"
I barked into the phone. It was only six months into our marriage when I first called a friend for legal advice. Andre and I had our first huge argument, and now I can't even remember what it was about. Funny how I can still remember how angry I was, though.

That argument didn't result in divorce proceedings, but six months later I left him anyway.

Disbelief and sadness overwhelmed me. And I was so confused! My family's advice ranged from telling me to

34

leave immediately to sticking it out. Then I began to doubt my decision. Was I jumping the gun? Would the situation escalate--now or later?

I couldn't believe my marriage was going to be over so soon! I didn't want to leave, but I decided that I had to in order to get my point across to Andre. For all the explaining I did, I felt like he still didn't understand that there was certain behavior that I *could* not and *would* not tolerate from him.

The decision to leave was made during an argument when an irate Andre had disconnected the phone while I was talking to my Mother. When he next turned off the electricity in the house, I called the Police. Not because I thought he would hurt me, but because I needed my electricity back on. My husband took the police officer's "suggestion" and resided at his Mother's house that night.

The next day when I told Andre that I had decided to leave him, he told me to get out immediately. We "negotiated," and he gave me two weeks to find another place to live. Less than 24 hours later, though, he shortened that to one week.

He even announced that he was going to start dating *and* bring his dates to the house--whether or not I was there!

35

I said fine; I'd be dating, too. In fact, I called one of my ex-boyfriends that night.

After that, I spent most of my time in the guest room. Meanwhile, Andre harassed me as much as he could. He was so intolerable, my pets and I went to stay with my sister after only two days.

I started looking for an apartment. I tried to seem impressed when the leasing agent showed me the closet I could afford, but it was hard. It wasn't long before I moved in the complex where my two sisters lived. Being with them helped me with the pain and isolation of leaving my man--maybe for a while, maybe for a lifetime. I really didn't know what the future held.

After our separation, it was at least two months before my husband and I had a conversation that didn't end in a screaming match. Whether we spoke in person or over the phone, we just weren't able to talk rationally. Even our first post-separation date ended horribly. Andre had called me to meet him for brunch at one of our favorite restaurants. It started out pretty well, but ended abruptly when he insulted me.

On our second date after I moved out, Andre offered some insight into what he thought contributed to our breakup. At the time I dismissed it, but the more I think about it, he may have been right. He said that I was bored.

He was right about the fact that we rarely had extra money, and therefore, we couldn't go anywhere. Like the weekend trip he promised we would take on our first anniversary that never came to pass. Maybe I *was* bored, but I was even more resentful of the way he spent money.

The minute I slept with him (our second post-separation date), he assumed I wanted to get back together. It just kind of happened, even though I really wasn't ready.

When my six-month apartment lease was up, I moved back to our home. Or should I say, *we* moved back home. I never did officially invite Andre to move in with me, but I spent only two months alone in my apartment. Meanwhile, he had rented our home to two of his co-workers.

Returning home, I didn't know what to expect. I was nervous; I knew I would miss my sisters, and I was worried about the condition of my home. When I walked in, however, my fears were eased. I thought I'd made the right decision to return home with my husband.

I didn't know if it would be forever, though. When Andre asked me to promise that I would never leave him again, I said, "I can't promise you that, Andre. Because if you ever verbally abuse me again, I'll leave you again."

Just for your information, Andre admitted that he didn't waste any time getting on the Internet for dates during our first separation. I really wasn't flattered by that, to tell you the truth. And then the fact that he had three different dates *with three different women* in only two months.

C-O-N-T-R-O-L

It's a seven-letter word with a seven billion dollar price tag. And even if *you* can afford it, your *marriage* can't. Why? Because it breeds hatred, resentment and everything bad.

It was actually the driving force behind the biggest problem in our marriage, which is verbal abuse. I never dreamed that the man who claimed to love me in so many ways would be capable of--much less *want* to--unleash such rage on me. It really was a surprise, and not a very good one. It's nothing like being cussed out by family and friends. It hurts more--a lot more. And it's *much* harder to believe.

If you must use bad words, take the personal attack out of them. Just listen to how much better, "*That* is stupid" sounds opposed to "*You* are stupid." Make no mistake; words *can* and *will* do irreparable harm to a relationship.

Yet, he continued to do it! One night he asked to borrow my bank card again. He needed gas for his truck and we both needed some Aspirin. Since I had $10 cash on me, I gave it to him with explicit instructions to use the cash for gas, and the Visa for the Aspirin. But did he? No. He came home and directed me to subtract $40 from my bank account. I said, "You bought $40 worth of Aspirin?!"

Why had he done the exact opposite of what I'd asked is what I wanted to know. *He* had decided that I needed the $10 cash for lunch the next day, so he charged everything on my Visa.

I explained to him that I didn't want any more checks out because my account was screwed up at the moment. He immediately exploded--calling me names and accusing *me* of hoarding money!

Knowing that the pets get nervous when we raise our voices, I just laid back down in bed and tried to go to sleep. But that wasn't enough for him. I finally had to threaten to sleep over at my sister's house before he would calm down.

A few months later, we decided to go out for Sunday brunch. We went to a Denny's restaurant and had a great time. Then on the drive home, all Hell broke loose. And all I did was "criticize" his driving. (I asked him to slow down because it was raining.) I forgot I'd agreed not to, but he soon reminded me. He was in a rage in an instant! He started yelling and lecturing and got so worked up that he scared me. That's when I decided to clam up and let him vent all his frustration.

I just sat there and wondered what the *real* problem was. Nobody goes *that* nuts over a little criticism. He told me to shut my ____ing mouth 17 times on the way home!

My husband never raised a hand to me, but he may as well have. The effect is the same. Shock, mental scars, hurt, disbelief, fear, mistrust and shattered dreams. The irony is that every time he tried to lower my self-esteem by belittling me, he was actually belittling himself in my eyes. The respect I had for him was chipped away every time he *chose* to do it. I can't recall a single time when I thought to myself that I deserved it. So why, is the question I kept asking myself.

But maybe I was going to all that trouble for nothing. Andre had known the answer all along. Imagine my surprise when he informed me that *I* made him do it!

Oh, really? He became my puppet? Obviously, I did not control him or his mouth. Nor would I want to. What I *expected* is that he cared enough about me that he would want to control *himself.*

He even tried to lay a guilt trip on me when I told him that I would leave him if he ever mistreated me again. *He accused me* of not taking our wedding vows seriously! Whereby I let him know that even God does not expect that one partner should ever be at the mercy of the other. There are some things in a marriage that are just plain deal-breakers, and abuse is one of them.

Heaven knows I didn't want to believe that I married an abuser. Among other things, it's embarrassing! That's why I tried to hide it at first; I tried to pretend it didn't happen. At the same time, I knew I would eventually tell my Mother about it. And other people too--I know how I am.

But maybe he wouldn't do it again. If *only* he wouldn't do it again, I would tell myself. I could forget the past and start afresh. I didn't want to leave my husband and an otherwise happy marriage.

To try to live with it, I tried to excuse it. The truth is, I can look to the ends of the Earth, but no excuse is good enough. Because along with being totally deliberate, the threat of what might trigger his anger was always with me. Subjecting another person to waiting and wondering if a simmering pot is going to boil over is nothing less than a form of cruelty. And that's just what it felt like.

The whole idea was to scare me into doing what he wanted--without question. Intimidation starts out as a cheap manipulation tool, but can wind up costing you your marriage. Not exactly a bargain in the long run.

I absolutely *hate* to admit it, but it got to the point where Andre could control me without saying a word. Just the memories of his past temper tantrums were enough to make me tiptoe around him like he was surrounded by land mines, and that's pathetic.

If I couldn't feel comfortable around my own husband, in my own home, that couldn't continue. There was nothing fair about it, but there *was* something good that came from the acknowledgment.

I felt like less of a person inside when I allowed Andre to replace my decisions with his. No way around it--I was being controlled. Once I admitted that to myself (not easy, by the way), I also knew he wasn't going to change his ways. After all, his approach was working for him. That left only one alternative.

I had to change *my* ways. I tried to put anger and resentment on the back burner and instead, concentrated on how I could avoid manipulation in the first place. A big job, and not one I'm sure I've found an answer for.

As I write this today, I still can't say I understand how a person thinks they can profit from abuse of any kind. And I'm wasting my time, anyway. The fact is, every time Andre spewed venom on me with his words, he made the decision to do it.

Repeat after me, "There's no excuse for verbal abuse." Keep that under your hat in case you ever need it. Too many of us will.

One time, for example, he decided to buy a new computer and printer. I asked him to wait until we got in a better financial position. But disregarding all logic, he paid over $1,000 for them--financed at a whopping 24% interest! It was a bad idea, but since it was *his* idea....

Another way my husband exerted control was by ignoring my input on how we spent *our* money. It took him about a year, but he finally admitted to me that the reason he was unwilling to relinquish his control of our money had to do with his ex-girlfriend. Andre said that he would beg his ex to let him handle their finances, but she refused. He didn't like it, but he did agree to it since she contributed the most financially to the household budget.

Here's the most devastating thing about my husband's need for control. If I let it, Andre's desire to manage *my* life would rip away my dreams. We battled constantly over my need to quit my nine to five job so I could devote more time to writing this book. Basically, Andre supported my ambition in life as long as it didn't jeopardize the security a second income affords.

I could understand his fear that he didn't want to be dead broke the way we were for the first eight months of our marriage, but not to the point where it stifled my hopes and dreams. And, too, any financial success I achieved would benefit us equally. He said he believed in me, so I wanted him to put his money where his mouth was.

Unfortunately, control comes in many forms, and I'm about to reveal some more. One by one, Andre came to place restrictions on me. So much so, that one day I yelled, "Why don't you just write me a rule book on how to be your wife?!"

"You need one!" he yelled back.

I doubt it! I have a mind of my own, and I didn't intend to stop using it just because I got married. I'm not one to be controlled, and I let him know it, too. Not that it stopped him.

I can't believe that Andre thought he had the right to tell me what I could and could not do. One time he told me I couldn't even so much as wave to the neighbors across the street. It made sense to him because *he* had it out with them. But the whole thing was *his* fault! Meanwhile, they were friends of mine. We argued until I realized he wasn't going to give in. I finally agreed to act as though they didn't exist.

After that, my contact with the neighbors was more infrequent, but it was a lot more interesting. Until they started telling me unflattering things about my husband that I already knew to be true. I learned to keep my conversations with them short and sweet.

But control can be more than someone making unreasonable demands of you. Sometimes, it's disguised as a favor. Here are a few I could have done without.

One day, Andre bought me a cellular phone that I didn't want or need. To go along with it, he bought 300 minutes of airtime. When I didn't use them, he increased the minutes to 500. When I didn't use those either, he "lost" them, and that's how it was all my fault.

In addition, the contract he signed with the phone company didn't allow him to cancel in his lifetime. That's *another* problem with only one person making all the decisions--some are non-retractable.

Andre was my hairdresser for a while, until I had to let him go. He got too picky about *he* wanted for *my* hair. He was already buying my conditioner as it was. It wasn't long before I had a years supply of whatever. I didn't even have storage for them all. Anyway, between that and his coloring advice, I'd had it. Ms. Clairol he isn't. He hadn't even colored his own hair!

Another time, Andre joined a book club. He ordered books for himself, and that was okay. He bought me a book on how to write and sell a novel and that was great;

I appreciated it. But then he got more books for me, and I was beginning to see a theme--sex, sex, sex!

What puzzled me the most is why he thought I needed him to select my reading material. He never did ask me what *I* wanted. He just kept ordering those books and presenting them as gifts. He claimed to be happy with our sex life, so I didn't understand it. It doesn't matter anyway; I never even opened them.

Andre continued his antics in what he thought were more subtle ways. For example, one night he came home and checked the messages on the answering machine. He told me there were two calls for me.

One call was from my Mother and he punched in the code and handed me the phone to listen to it. The other call was from my sister--which he had already erased! I asked him what gave him the right to delete a message I hadn't even heard and he said that the message wasn't important. That earned him a 15-minute lecture on simple respect.

Having to struggle for control over my own life is not how I want to live. I learned to set limits for *everybody*-- including my husband. I had to watch him or he would have been bossing me around left and right. He even laughed when I called him on it because he knew what he was doing was wrong. If you suspect that your spouse is trying to take advantage of you, they probably are. *Do something about it!*

Damage Control.

I'll never forget this one woman who wrote to Ann Landers complaining that her husband would drive 85 miles an hour while reading the newspaper. She wanted advice on how to get him to stop it. I can't remember the answer given by the queen of advice, but I can give you my own personal understanding on how to control your husband. Not!

Andre did something *very* stupid one weekend and there was little I could do about it. He got upset with our neighbor and stood in our front yard screaming across the street at him. I tried to get him to stop by pleading with him and tried to grab his arm. He only got louder and angrier as he brushed past me.

What followed was the kind of anger that comes wickedly fast--picking up steam as it escalates. I could have tried to out-yell him. Knowing him as I do, though, I left the scene. I immediately went inside the house so at least he wouldn't have an audience. He came in soon after and wondered why I wouldn't speak to him.

When I finally did speak to him several hours later, I told him he had embarrassed me, the neighbors, and most of all himself by his ridiculous and unnecessary performance. He said he didn't give a damn about the neighbors, but apologized to me. An apology wasn't going to do me any good; what I wanted was for him to stop doing it.

It's no fun trying to stay one step ahead of an idiot. But that's what damage control is all about, as this next story illustrates.

It was a Saturday night and we had plans to meet Andre's co-workers for dinner at a restaurant located 50 miles from our home. I didn't even want to go, but he insisted. I decided to join him, but I did ask that he limit his intake of alcohol so he wouldn't be driving drunk on the way home.

Well, I was immediately chastised for trying to ruin his evening with my "nagging." He said that this was his first chance to be with his friends from his new job and he was going to enjoy it. He assured me that he wasn't going to get drunk; he was just going to have a good time.

I wanted to believe that, but I also wanted to remind him that he had a warrant out for his arrest. A warrant that was for his failure to show up in court for an expired inspection sticker he received while driving my car. (I told you I procrastinate!) Anyway, he didn't want to hear it, so to keep the peace, I dropped the subject. Except to ask him to *at least* refrain from speeding on the drive home.

Speaking of the drive home, right after we were pulled over (for speeding), my husband was given a sobriety test--which he promptly flunked. He had been told to recite the alphabet and he came up one letter short. Mercifully, he was given another chance and passed. The situation ended unexpectedly when the officer got called to a robbery that was in progress and left in a hurry. He took one last look at my husband and said, "Try not to kill anybody on your way home."

When I think of what could have happened, I get livid. I regret the irresponsibility on the part of us both. Andre for insisting on operating a 3,000 pound vehicle while drunk, and me for not sharing the global responsibility of safe driving. Looking back, I could have--and should have--completely abstained from drinking that night, knowing my husband's past behavior. He usually does what he wants, and that night was no exception.

From that little "disaster-waiting-to-happen," I learned that you can't control another person's behavior--even if it is for their own good. Understand that there's only so much you can do if your spouse is intent on acting the fool. Having a Plan B (like staying overnight in a local bed and breakfast) could be your only salvation.

Stop the Stresses!

People are worried about everything from their sagging behinds (I know more than one) to the ozone level in the Earth's atmosphere. I've got my worries too, but since I've changed my focus from worrying to problem-solving, I feel more in control and better able to cope with life.

Just because a problem is dropped in your lap doesn't mean you can't eliminate it, minimize its effect, or even benefit from it. But you *do* have to take some action. Even if it's just to change your way of thinking. I did, and here's what happened.

About ten years ago, I was very depressed because I didn't see a very bright future for myself. I was also traumatized after my young brother, with whom I was very close, died unexpectedly. I was painfully shy and had stomach problems constantly due to stress. The mere mention of a staff meeting at work sent me running to the restroom.

I was also getting older and desperately wanted to find a man who was marriage material. I had some great boyfriends, but the ones I wanted to marry didn't want to marry me. I didn't even have any girlfriends to go out with so I could meet more men.

I was working as a secretary in a large school district with a supervisor determined to make my life a living hell until she could fire me. I liked my job and co-workers, but the supervisor made me want to quit. Since I was living paycheck to paycheck, though, quitting wasn't an option. I thought about suicide a lot.

The day I changed my attitude was the day I changed my life. I was so tired of working just to pay the bills, I decided to do something about it. I didn't stop grieving for my brother, but I did gain a new determination to succeed--with his help.

I began with the decision to finish my college education. I knew if I made more money, I could afford to go on vacation and meet men. But that was just a side dish. The main course was going to benefit me for the rest of my life. Even if nothing else came from it (like a better job or more pay), I would know that I accomplished a goal.

So after a 12-year absence from college, I went back to school and got my bachelor's degree in English. I worked all day and went to school at night for the next three and

...me that when something happens to disrupt my ...n, I will simply work around it. Consciously ...things in perspective has drastically lowered my ...vel.

...unterbalance Stress...

...and I found joy in the little things. For example, ...f the happiest moments of our day occurred when ...usband came home from work. Our puppy went ... She howled and danced and jumped in Daddy's ...s. After he held her for a while, she ran all around the ...m bouncing off the furniture. She was hilarious to ...ch! It wasn't a *big* moment, but it was a *bright* moment, ...d we looked forward to it.

...ress comes without invitation, but relaxation must be ...ought. We all have our coping mechanisms, and it's not ...selfish to use them. In fact, it's imperative we do use ...them. When I need a break from life, I take to my bed. ...It's my think tank. I need to have quiet solitude to solve ...my problems. And to get away from them.

...I also relax when I'm creating. Whether it's writing, ...making a floral arrangement or decorating the house, I ...forget about all my troubles. And I can always find peace ...while soaking in a warm bath with candles aglow. Add a ...glass of wine and it's all good.

---

a half years. I hated it so bad that sometimes I'd drive all the way downtown to the university and not even go to class. It wasn't easy, but it *was* worth it.

While in school, I met one of the best friends I've ever had. One day I was complaining to him that I would never find a husband. He happened to own a barter business and gave me a free membership to a video dating service. About six months later, I visited the club and another great change occurred in my life.

Not only did I meet several great men with whom I had long relationships, I also made a lot of male and female friends. Friendships that last to this day. My social life stepped up tenfold, and I wasn't lonely anymore.

Things were definitely looking up in my personal life, but the time came when I could no longer take the harassment at work. I felt forced to leave the job I'd had for nine years. All my security went out the window while I lived on my retirement benefit of $13,000 and then my credit cards. But I stayed in school. And now, I could--and did--increase my hours.

At 37, I earned my college degree exactly 20 years after my graduation from high school. Indisputably, one of the best decisions I've ever made. Here's one reason why.

In lieu of a final exam, my professor of Greek Mythology required a lengthy term paper. I felt good about the essay I'd written on Elizabethan Theatre, but I never expected what happened next.

For the first time in her career (she told me), this professor called a student at home. And that student was me. She told me how impressed she was with my work and even shared it with her husband. Her exact words were, "It was a joy to read."

That was a defining (lightbulb) moment for me. For the first time in my life, I thought that maybe--just maybe--I could be a professional writer. Her words gave me confidence and encouragement, and I will never forget them. Obviously, they had a great effect on me because here you are reading a book that I wrote!

Finishing college triggered an upward trend in my life that's continued ever since. Even the panic attacks I began suffering after my brother's death eventually led me to a doctor who gave me Prozac. To say it changed my life would be an understatement. The first thing I noticed was that it all but eliminated my shyness! Suddenly, I felt much more relaxed with other people and within my own skin. And a lot happier. One friend of mine astounded me

when he told me he no personality! I didn't think

During this time, I also manufacture stress. Now categories--minor and major. I realistic assessment of a situatio end. Is it reversible? Can it alternative? Is the world goin happens?

Well, one day something did happen a sudden I couldn't leave my bed, let or work. Everything in my life stopp weeks. During that time, I found indispensable at work as I thought I was. make good grades and miss three weeks of

Not only did my life not fall apart the way I might, but my family and friends came to my parents came in from out of town and Moth and cleaned for me. My sister washed my h bathtub because I was too weak to do it mys although I missed many classes, my professors with me to get caught up.

It taught
life's pla
keeping
stress le

To C
Andre
one o
my
nuts
arm
roo
wa
an

It's hard to say what Andre did to release pressure. I'm afraid his only outlet may have been complaining to his friends at work, and that wasn't enough. I know he didn't confide in his family because he didn't want them to know our business. In fact, the reason they knew as much as they did was because of me.

There is one thing, however, that Andre and I did together that relieved stress. No, it wasn't sex. Well, maybe for him. But I'm talking about how much we laughed. Between us, we could find the humor in almost everything.

We teased each other constantly--and mercilessly. I thought it was hysterical when he said he was going to get rid of me the next day because it was heavy trash day. And he cracked up when I suggested he get a social security number for his nose so we could claim another deduction on our taxes. When you share the same sense of humor with your spouse, it's better than Valium.

When lemons turn into lemonade, it's because *we* make it so. When Andre and I both lost our jobs at the onset of our marriage, instead of cursing our bad luck we took advantage of the time the situation afforded us. I knew there was a lifetime of work just waiting for us and I was worked long hours because she worked with him, yet she imposed on *my* husband to be her own personal maintenance man? I guarantee you he fixed the last of her stuff for a long time to come. I don't mind helping other people, but there's a limit. Especially when it involves *my* husband.

Psycho Exes.

It all started when this half-woman, half-wolf found out I was dating her ex-husband. I'll call him Al.

During my courtship with this man (two years before I met my husband), my two sisters and I had moved into the house Al formerly shared with his family. A house that was awarded to him in their divorce settlement.

Even though the rent was free, the decision was costly. "Hell hath no fury like a woman scorned!" describes this piece of work to a tee. Forget the fact that she and Al had been divorced for five years *and* she lived with another man, she was out for blood.

This 48-year-old punk pulled some doozies. She stole our mail, including the $200 in cash my Mother sent to my sister. When we put a lock on the mailbox, she stole the entire box and left the two sticks standing by the curb! She cut down the bushes in the front yard, and Christmas